I0488271

More Life, Less Work:

45 Simple Strategies to Achieve Maximum Productivity and Success

A.C. Jones

Table of Contents

Introduction

Every business needs to maximize on its productivity if they want to be successful. It's therefore imperative for a company to understand how to utilize its resources with maximum efficiency. This is because if a company is productive, it benefits the owners, employees, and customers. Everyone wins. Not only do customers gain great customer service and better interaction with the business, the owners of the company also gain a profit, which is the ultimate goal. Meanwhile the employees gain other incentives, such as praise, usually in the form of a raise or a bonus.

There are many different strategies that can help you to maintain a productive business. This book focuses on 45 different ones. They are broken down based on time, organization, goals and bad habits.

Time has to be managed to maintain productivity. It's important to prioritize and avoid procrastination. Using the 80/20 rule, businesses can focus on the little bit that will make the most impact. Taking breaks and following the Two Minute Rule will also help to keep momentum going, while deadlines help to hold people accountable for their work.

Goals are important in defining what is important to the business. They need to be analyzed and assessed for validity. By choosing to define goals for the business from the outset, this will personally help to keep people motivated. Whenever goals are not meeting our expectations, it's important to adjust them.

The final aspect of productivity is finding a way to stay up to date. Businesses need to check their software and train their employees. Employees may also need to further their education and knowledge beyond what the business hands out.

After reading this book, you will be able to find ways to maximize your productivity within your organization. You will find ways to help others be more efficient and productive for the sake of the company. You will also be able to offer suggestions for the company to utilize its resources to the best of their ability.

Productivity should be of the utmost important to businesses and individuals...considering every business is made up of individuals, the success relies on every part being on the same page. They should have the same goals and be working toward the same level of efficiency.

Use this book as a guide - by following the 45 strategies inside you can learn how to start your business on the pathway to maximum productivity. Now all you have to do is implement them!

To your business success,

A.C. Jones

1. Time Management

Time management is important because we only have so much of it. As it's not infinite, we have to make the best use of the time we have to be as efficient and productive as possible. If we find a way to manage our time correctly, we can get more done in less time. When you manage your time well, you create *extra* time for yourself. This will allow you to learn more. You can have more time to relax and breathe, meaning you will find yourself feeling less stressed. Time management can also improve your organizational and preparation skills. You will find that your work is of a higher quality. All of these collectively, allow you a better chance of being success.

If someone has poor time management skills, they are more likely to follow detrimental patterns that decrease efficiency and productivity. People that are often late to scheduled events have poor time management. It's possible that they won't be late, but they are rushing all the time. The most common mismanagement of time is procrastination. That is the practice of putting tasks off until the last minute. This increases a person's amount of stress and decreases their quality of work. Believe it or not, agreeing to everything is poor time management. Quality time management will include delegating, delaying, or even deleting certain tasks that are unimportant.

Here is an example of lacking quality time management.

Robert arrives to work 5 minutes late. He doesn't worry about it because he is not docked pay until 6 minutes. He sits at his desk and starts answering emails. During his email quest, he comes across some topics that warrant some internet searches. He's been at work for 3 hours now and has barely begun his list of tasks. After starting some daily items, he looks up and realizes it is time for lunch. When he returns from lunch, he looks over the amount of work he needs to complete. It seems overwhelming. Robert starts to finish off tasks at a hurried pace. Some items are done at a decreased level of quality, but they get done.

Here is an example of using quality time management.

Robert arrives to work 5 minutes early. He knows that his boss is very appreciative of his timeliness. He sits at his desk and glances over his emails for any immediate concerns. There are 4 items he responds to instantly. He begins his daily items and completes them in the next hour. Finally, he completes his daily regimen by answering the remaining emails. Several of the items need to be forwarded to other members of the company for completion. By lunchtime, he is almost completed with all pending work. Robert is now prepared to complete items in preparation for tomorrow and the weekly meeting on Friday.

2. Mind Maps

Mind maps are a creative way to organize a task list. It helps with time management, organization, and prioritization. A mind map looks like a tree of ideas or tasks centered around one major concept. They are interactive and change throughout your day or work. The more creative you are with your mind map the more beneficial it will be. You might want to consider using multiple colors or pictures to draw your attention to a particular topic or theme.

Creating a mind map allows you to use both your right and left side of the brain, which produces better results. Using a mind map will help you to manage your time more effectively and also helps to break a large project or task into much smaller, more manageable tasks. It is also recognized that mind maps help to improve memory and learning.

On the next page you will see an example of an effective mind map.

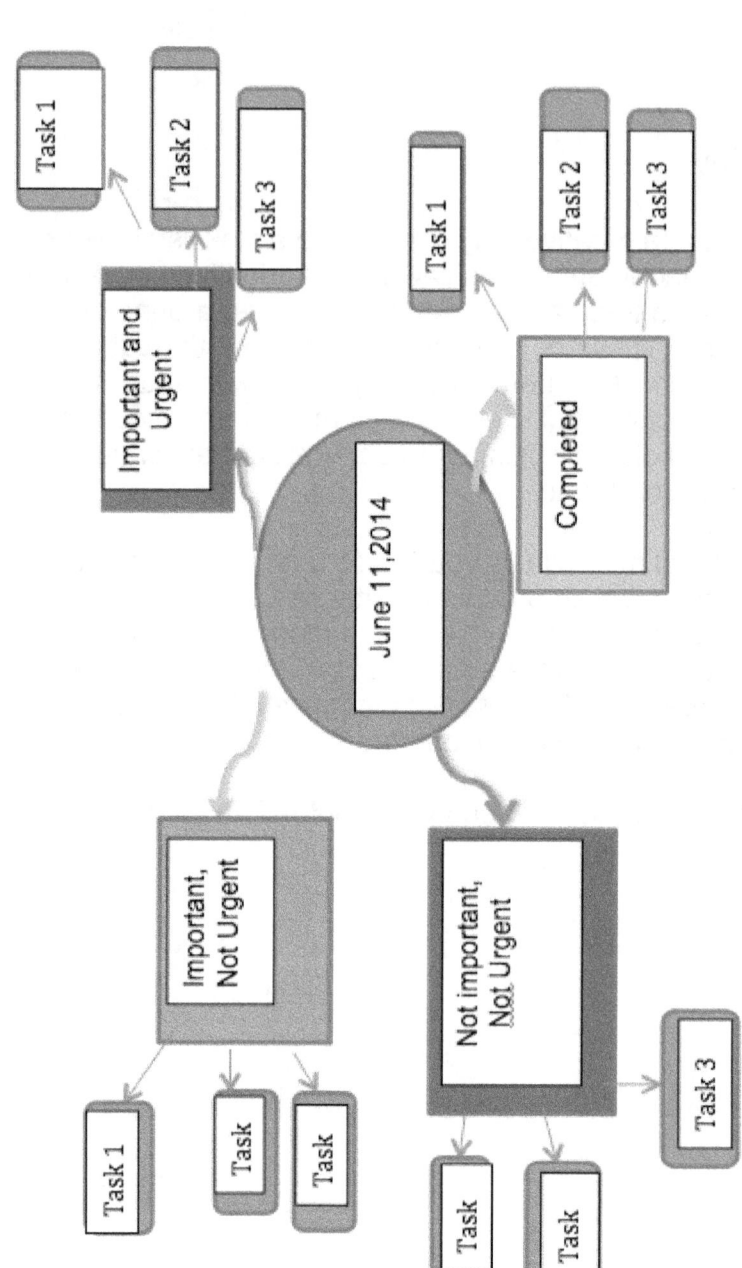

3. Organization

Organization is import to productivity. There are different things that should be considered in someone's organizational skills. They usually always involve papers. Find out what kind of papers you have and get them sorted into categories. Look at a person's capability to find something quickly. Look at all your things, including papers and find 8-10 categories that exist. As time management is a part of being organized, someone that is organized should have a definitive way of recording tasks and time.

Being disorganized can cause a person to feel overwhelmed. The clutter can take over a person's life. You can change your organizational habits. Start with sorting. Establish a place for each grouping; it can be files or boxes.

Get rid of items that no longer have a purpose. It doesn't mean you have to throw them out. Simply remove them from your work area. Consider placing them in storage if they have some value in the long run. Use a filing system to categorize your files or groups together. The biggest issue is maintaining that system. It's very easy to get a system started, but harder to follow through.

Find a way to schedule maintaining your organizational system. You should plan on daily or weekly filing. A rule of thumb for placing items is items you deal with daily should be on your desk. If there are things you use weekly, they go in your desk. Anything that is touched monthly should be near your desk.

Here's an example of overlooking organization.

Robert is approached by his boss. He has a new client that he would like to show his presentation to. He asks Robert to bring him the presentation. Robert has a hard copy somewhere in his cubicle. He shuffles around the papers on his desk. He looks through his recycle bag. He continues to search high and low. There is no designated place for it. He calls his boss and informs him that he has been unable to locate a copy of the presentation. It is clear from his boss's tone that he is unhappy. Robert returns to his work. After several hours, he finds the presentation in the middle of a binder he has. He takes the presentation to his boss's office. The meeting is over and the boss no longer needs the presentation. Robert is dismissed.

Here's an example of using great organizational skills.

Robert is approached by his boss. He has a new client that he would like to show his presentation to. He asks Robert to bring him the presentation. Robert has a hard copy available. He walks to his bookshelf. He removes the binder labeled, "New Lines". He flips to the back of the binder to find the newest material. He removes his copy and walks to the copy machine. He makes a new clean copy that the new client can take with him. His boss is happy and satisfied with his performance. When the client leaves, his boss approaches Robert and tells him that things went well. He states that he couldn't have done it without his help.

4. Focus on Goals

Goals are important to productivity. Having goals increases a person's level of performance. It serves as motivation and allows a person to credit themselves with satisfaction from their performance. A person can use their goals to determine if they are successful. Goals help to direct your efforts. They can be used to increase your performance, especially if a goal in to increase your output. A goal can be used to motivate a person through obstacles. They can also drive a person to change their bad habits.

Effective goal setting requires using SMART goals. SMART stands for Specific, Measureable, Assignable, Realistic, and Time Related. This means that you have be detailed about what you want to achieve. Avoid being vague, or you may achieve your goal without really doing any favors. Make sure that your goal can be measured for success. Find out who the goal can be assigned to, or who is needed to complete your goal. It can be easy to make goals unrealistic. These are dreams, not goals. Finally, every goal needs to have a deadline.

Here's an example of a SMART goal. Robert has been working for the company for 3 years. He has evaluated a new goal. He wants to receive a management position.

S: Specific. Robert wants a management position within his company.

M: Measurable. A management position would be offered in writing by his upper management.

A: Assignable. In order to get this position, he would need to perform to his best. He would need to have upper management aware of his desire for the position. He would also need his boss to retire, as he has discussed.

R: Realistic. Robert has a bachelor's degree, which is required. He has the experience with the business from his current position. In the past, he was a manager at a retail store, which gives him management experience. It is realistic for Robert to obtain a management position within the company.

T: Time Related. His boss is expected to retire within the next 6 months. Therefore, Robert has a goal of achieving this position within the next 9 months.

5. Fight Procrastination

Procrastinating is putting off tasks until the last minute. A person may choose to procrastinate because they are angry at having to complete the task to begin with. They may be uninterested in the task. Procrastination creates feelings of guilt and stress. It's not unusual that those that procrastinate are unorganized. The tasks pile up.

One of the dangers of procrastination includes missing out on opportunity. It's common for someone to feel guilty about putting off their tasks, to the point where they then have to go beyond their original call of duty to get the work done. Procrastinating can also hurt relationships. In response to feeling guilty, it's common to avoid the person assigning the task that was procrastinated over and even hand the work in past a specific deadline or in an incomplete state, which looks unprofessional.

You can start to combat procrastination by changing the way you think. Say to yourself that you will complete the task. Get started. Gather all necessary tools before starting. This will eliminate any reduction in momentum that may be created when a particular tool is missing. Make a schedule dividing your tasks, as this will help keep you accountable for your work. Keep yourself realistic. You have spent a lifetime building a habit of procrastinating. It will not disappear overnight. Ensure that you keep your deadlines realistic and that you prioritize your tasks. You can do this by making sure that you focus on tasks that matter.

Here is an example of overlooking the habit of procrastination.

Robert has accepted an assignment at work that requires him to work overnight at home. He starts the drive home and remembers that the season finale of his favorite series is on tonight. He arrives home at 6:00. He makes his dinner and eats. It's now 7:00. He has one hour until his show comes on. He looks at the task of his assignment and knows that one hour will not give him much progress. He sits on the couch and opens his computer to check his social media accounts. An hour has passed and his show is starting. Once the show is complete, it is now 9:00. Robert pulls out his work and gets started. It is common for him to go to bed by 11:00. At 11:00, he is not even half way through the work. The final work is due first thing the next morning. He has to stay up until 3:00 am to complete the work. When he arrives at work the next day, he is tired. He looks a mess and is having trouble focusing. The work he completed is disorganized, due to Robert being so tired when he completed it. It was done in a hurry and isn't his best work.

Here is an example of avoiding procrastination.
Robert has accepted an assignment at work that requires him to work overnight at home. He starts the drive home and remembers that the season finale of his favorite series is on tonight. He arrives home at 6:00. He makes his dinner and eats. It's now 7:00. He has 1 hour until his show starts. He sits at the TV and programs his DVR or TiVo to record the episode so that he can watch it tomorrow. He sits at the table and gathers all his supplies for the work. Without any distraction, he is finished by 10:00. He finishes tired, but it's not too bad. He gets everything ready to take to work tomorrow and heads to bed.

When he wakes the next day, he is well rested and prepared to hand in his work. He arrives on time and looks good. His boss glances over the project, which is organized and well done. His boss will remember the outcome of his work when new opportunity presents itself.

6. Jumping Hurdles

When we speak of hurdles, we are really talking about the many obstacles presented before us. There are so many obstacles that can hinder our productivity. The first step of avoiding them is to identify them. Procrastination is one such detrimental obstacle. It's the process of putting things off until the last minute, with the results being stress filled and rushed. A person's performance suffers and the mental effects of being stressed are undesirable.

Perfectionism is an obstacle. Many people think that perfectionism is something that a company of business would desire. However, spending an excessive amount of time on details throughout a task that may or may not increase its outcome can be very unproductive. Interruptions are an obvious obstacle. Phone calls, emails, or coworkers can be interruptive to our work. It's important to find an environment that removes these interruptions to improve productivity.

There are multiple ways to eliminate hurdles from your work. You can start by challenging yourself. Remember to encourage improvement. Avoid striving for perfectionism. Think more along the lines of completing a task instead of picking at it continuously. Identify what obstacles you face and find a plan of action to remove them. Everyone and every environment can be faced with different obstacles.

Here's an example of a task filled with obstacles.

Robert sits at his desk and has several hours before an important meeting. He knows that he has to have the agenda completed very quickly. He starts the document and receives a phone call. After dealing with the call, a half hour has passed. He gets back to the agenda and finds himself constantly backtracking for corrections and improvements. Robert is down to one hour remaining before the meeting and his coworker stops for a chat. The discussion is longer than it should be. It is time for the meeting and Robert hurriedly puts together an incomplete agenda and heads there.

Here's an example of avoiding obstacles.

Robert sits at his desk and has several hours before an important meeting. He knows that he has to have the agenda completed very quickly. He starts the document and receives a phone call. He answers the call, takes down details and assures the caller that he will handle it by the end of the day. Very little time was lost and he continues creating the agenda. He starts with an outline and adds some details for each item. He fills in which people will be responsible for each item. His coworker approaches his desk. After a very brief hello, Robert lets him know that he will have to catch up with him later. The agenda is completed two hours before the meeting and has sufficient information for a productive meeting.

7. Balancing Work and Play

It's important to maintain a balance of work and play to continue to be productive. Too much of either can be damaging. If you are playing too much, obviously your work will suffer. It will show on your performance and those that sign your paycheck will not be happy. If you have all work and no play, your social life and state of mind will suffer. People only reach out so many times to try and get together with you. If you are constantly turning them away, they'll stop asking. When the work goes away, you'll find yourself alone. It's also possible that your work will suffer because the amount of stress increases when your life is full of work. Play can be a way of decompressing that stress that is created from work.

There are many ways to try and balance work and play. Make sure that you live in an area that you are happy with. When the workday ends, you are left to your environment to stay entertained. If you hate the area you live in, you are more likely to continue working or avoid playtime. Stay passionate about multiple things. Find a way to get organized. If you are organized and manage your time appropriately, you will have more time for play. Plan vacations ahead of time. Look forward to your playtime.

Here's an example of failing to balance work and play.

Robert has become quite the overachiever. He brings his work home with him. When his day ends, he sits down on his couch and continues to work. His friends have called and asked him to go out. However, he has turned them down because he is sitting in front of the computer. Eventually, his friends stop asking. Robert is beginning to become more and more stressed about work. Your job, which was once fun, has now consumed your life. Instead of being prepared and dedicated to his workday, he dreads walking into the building.

Here's an example of finding the right balance of work and play.

Robert works during normal business hours with impressive time management skills and organization. When the day ends, he goes to the gym and works out. He has a passion for music. Often, during the weekends, he goes to different live shows to watch bands perform. There are many times that he invites his friends to come along. When the workday begins, he is still happy to have his job. He enters the building prepared and dedicated to completing his work. His level of stress is relatively low and does not come home with him at the end of the day.

8. Delegating

Delegation is important for productivity and efficiency. It allows tasks to be matched up with people who have matching skill sets. This frees you up to complete tasks that are more meant for your skill set. It also helps to encourage others to continue to develop their skills.

When you delegate tasks, it frees your time up for higher priority items. Items that are urgent but not important should be delegated. Sharing the responsibility with others helps to build confidence in them. If you are willing to trust them to complete the task, they feel needed and empowered. They grow in their knowledge level and self-esteem.

You want to trust in the right people. Find someone you can trust to complete the task without having to hold their hand through the process. Training should be done in the beginning. From then on, they should be able to follow through without to many questions. Consider the person's feelings who is receiving the task. They may be resentful or proud. Make sure that you are delegating the task to someone who should be completing it. This will eliminate the resentment. Don't choose a task to delegate because you don't want to do it yourself. Explain why you think they are good for the task and then be consistent about delegating tasks to these particular people.

Here's an example of delegating effectively.

Robert looks through his tasks for the day. There are several phone calls to be made. He has some reports that need to be completed and then sent out throughout the company. The information for the reports is already prepared. Robert is hosting a meeting. He has to have copies made of the agenda and some much needed materials. The list is becoming overwhelming. After looking over everything, he calls the receptionist. He asks her if she has enough time to make copies for a meeting while he finishes the reports. The reports are finished and he has phone calls to make. He emails the reports to his subordinate and calls her. He would like her to email the reports throughout the company. This will allow him to finish phone calls and get to the meeting on time.

9. *Teamwork*

Teamwork is a great tool for being productive and efficient. It allows tasks to be completed quicker. Working together can decrease the workload for individuals. It will also create happier employees, because no individual is without help or resources. This leaves them with less stress about their work. Working as a team builds relationships among workers. It makes it easier to ask for feedback or criticism. Teamwork increases trust among each other. This is because when you are part of a team, you hold yourself more accountable for your work. You do not want to be the one to let your team down. It also makes it easier to learn from others - let's face it, it is very rare that there is one person that is great at everything. We all have our strengths and weaknesses. It's beneficial to team together to let everyone exercise their strengths.

Teamwork can begin with programs that provide recognition. The workplace can coordinate social activities that allow people to bond and connect. Tasks can be broken down and distributed to specific individuals. It's also important that any disconnects in the team be addressed. Start by looking at the shortcomings of any particular person and developing ways to keep them on point. For example, if someone is notorious for not being prepared with their portion of a project, then create a timeline that they need to inform of their progress along the way. This will help keep them on track and eliminate any surprises.

Here's an example of effective teamwork.

Robert has recognized a problem with the company's customer service. He has called an emergency meeting. Robert starts the meeting and informs every one of the problem. They sit together and brainstorm ideas. Finally, they go through each idea and assess the validity and effects of carrying out the idea.

Each individual shares how the idea will affect their department. There are good and bad outcomes. Once each idea has been discussed, the team selects the best option. They create a plan to enforce the change and find an appropriate time for implementing it. They also create a follow up meeting.

Robert had no idea how to fix the problem. However, as a team, they found a solution and a plan to implement it. They also communicated among each other to find a solution that would do as little damage as possible throughout the company.

10. Consistency

Consistency is being predictable, and reliable. To be consistent, you have to do the same thing to receive the same results over and over again. Obviously, you want to be consistent with things that provide good results. Not the ones that provide negative or poor results. Ultimately, consistency results in a good reputation.

Any business wants to be consistent in the way they look. They want to deliver a great first impression. It's also important to treat your customers in a positive manner. The way you treat customers and employees needs to be consistent. They should know that they can count on great service every time. A company that is inconsistent will leave the customer wondering how they will be treated with each transaction. The act of wondering may lead them to a more reliable and consistent competitor. Consistency is important with follow through. If promises are made, they should be lived up to.

Here's an example of inconsistency hurting productivity.

Robert's company starts to push a new line of products. The sales people are out full force with the items. There are a few orders that come in.

After processing the orders, upper management decides that they make a better profit in certain areas. They want to exclude sales in other areas because of the reduced profit margin. The customers that are ordering the items are in the area that is cut out.

When they try and reorder, they are pushed away without an acceptable reason. The inconsistency leads them away from current and future orders. They cannot rely on the company and no longer want to do business with them.

Here's an example of consistent results increasing productivity.

Robert's company starts to push a new line of products. The sales people are out full force with the items. The customers know that they are getting what is promised from the company. They have always been upfront and honest. They have always delivered what is promised.

11. Accountability

Accountability is when you have to answer for your actions and results. People tend to talk a lot about holding people accountable. However, it is very easy to become defensive when that accountability is applied. Some companies use performance expectations to hold their employees accountable. To hold yourself accountable, you cannot get stuck with excuses. It's also important that when you are held accountable, there are specific repercussions to falling short of your goals.

To start being accountable for your own work, remember that you have to be responsible for the outcome whether the results are good or bad. It is easy to take the credit when things work out. However, it is much harder when things go downhill. Be empowered to make a move on things before someone gives you the permission. Remember that you can say no. Don't wait for others to recognize your efforts. Make sure that they know your good work. Make no excuses.

Don't lie to make a situation look better. Use self-reflection to make yourself accountable from time to time. Look to yourself for changing things in a positive way, instead of trying to change others. It's also important to listen to what others say about your performance. Criticism can be difficult, but if used the right way, you can be very productive.

12. Analysis

There are so many aspects to maintaining productivity. None of it matters if you don't stop every so often and analyze where you are at. There are times where changes are needed. The analysis identifies those areas. It helps to recognize what does and does not improve overall performance.

Any business may want to analyze the reliability of their staff. Find out if there is an increased amount of turnover and why. No one wants to put money into employees over and over and have them walk out the door. This leaves you starting over again. Analyze the tools that the employees are using. Are they up to date and efficient? Are there easy ways to make things more efficient?
Analysis is important for a company to decide what changes are needed. It is also important for individuals to see their own goals.

It's important to analyze the place that you work for. Is it right for you? Are your goals obtainable at this company? Do you waste most of your free time commuting when you could be doing the same thing much closer to home? Are there steps that you need to improve upon to stand out as a star employee? Each individual aspect of your career or success can be analyzed.

Here's an example of analyzing your time management.
Start by documenting how your time is spent. Consider keeping a journal or diary. Consider asking someone else to record your time. We sometimes omit things to make us look better when we do it ourselves. Find items that are unnecessary. Cut out items and tasks that are nonproductive. Eliminate distractions by assigning tasks larger blocks of time.

13. Believe in Your Success

Do you remember the story of the Little Train that Could? Everyone thought it was hopeless. They thought that it was impossible for the train to make it up the hill. He started out and said, "I think I can, I think I can."

This applies to the real world. It's important to believe in yourself. Negative self-talk can be a very powerful obstacle to being successful, productive and efficient. It wastes time and drags us down. We use self-talk to calm ourselves.

Here are some ways to find a way to believe in you and avoid negative self-talk.
Consider journaling. Summarize your feelings. Jot down any negative comments you think about yourself. This will allow you to look back and see the ridiculousness of the comments. Reprimand yourself for negative thoughts.

Make a conscious effort to stop those thoughts. Try wearing a rubber band around your wrist. Give it a snap for every negative thought or comment.

Replace it with a positive one, one that shows that you believe in yourself.

Change negative thoughts into questions. For example, "This is impossible!" becomes, "Is this impossible?"

Think it through and find a way to start believing in yourself.

14. Count the Pennies

Being sensible about money goes a long way in being productive. People that enjoy their work and are passionate can forget that at the end of the day it is a business. Everything we do costs money. The tools we use to complete a job costs money. The time that we spend completing a task costs the company money.

It's important to remember when completing each and every task that we are making it worthwhile. It is very easy to decrease productivity by wasting time, spending too many supplies on a task, or even literally giving things away, at the expense of making a profit.

Every task should be looked at for its money sense. The economy affects everyone and should be noted by every part of a team. It is possible to have a great company, with great employees, wonderful service and be completely broke because someone lost sight of the pennies. Productivity doesn't mean just keeping busy. It's important to be productive in making the company successful. For most companies, this usually means making a profit.

Watching what we spend within a company makes sense for everyone. It is sometimes easy to spend someone else's money. However, that money is what pays your paycheck. This is one of the reasons why it's important that you are making it worthwhile for you to be there.

Here are some examples of using good money sense to help the business.
Consider recycling. There are items that cost less because they are recycled. When purchasing equipment, consider using used equipment. It will cost less and can have the same functionality of new items.

A lot of companies spend a lot of money on advertising that doesn't bring in any customers. Make sure that all of your efforts are paying off.

Finally, before proposing an idea, consider the full cost of implementing it. When possible, bargain shop to keep costs down.

15. Find the Right Space

The space that you work in serves many purposes. It helps determine how productive you can be. It also tells people a lot about you. There are many people who claim to have an organized mess for a desk.

When it comes to your workspace, you shouldn't have to remember where something is. Instead, you should know where it belongs. This is easy because a productive workspace has a place for everything and everything is in its place.

Besides clutter, it's important to make sure that your space has enough room for all of your tools. It is too hard to have a space for everything if there literally isn't enough space. Clutter can cause stress and discomfort. The idea of having too much in too little space can be overwhelming and distracting to productivity.

Here's an example of a workspace that promotes productivity. Keep furniture that is movable. If something changes or you need a change it will be easy. Keep it clean. Find a way to stay private. It may be facing away from everyone or being in sight of a door or window.

Every office needs an area where everyone can work together or just be together. This can be a break room or a conference room. Be sure that the lighting is enough. Try and find a way to keep the noise to a minimum. Plants help to improve air quality, reduce noise, and please the eyes.

16. Prioritize

The act of prioritizing is placing things in an order by their level of importance. This is very important to being successful and productive. We are in a time where every person holds many hats. Every day proposes an infinite amount of tasks to be completed. If we don't' find a way to prioritize those tasks, we may never accomplish anything of any value. When we prioritize effectively, we save time and efforts. Effective prioritization maintains order within chaos, reduces a person's stress level, and finds a way to completion.

A common method of prioritizing is using the ABC method. All A items are vitally important. If these items are not completed there are consequences. It's important to complete these tasks on time no matter what. This may mean staying after or working extra hours. B items are important. They should be completed but have some wiggle room when it comes to the deadline. C items are optional. These can be tasks for future projects. They may have a deadline that is far away.

There are many ways to prioritize. You can create a list that spells it out. There are also many different digital apps that help document and prioritize our tasks.

Here's an example of poor prioritizing.

Robert comes into the office for the day. There are many tasks he has to complete. A meeting next week needs to have a presentation completed. There are reports due by the end of the day. Daily activities need to be completed.

Throughout the day, Robert works steadfast and hard. He completes the daily activities and then starts the presentation because he wants to get it done. However, at the end of a stressful day, he finds himself still needing to complete his reports and with no time to do it.

Here's an example of prioritizing.

Robert comes into the office for the day. There are many tasks he has to complete. A meeting next week needs to have a presentation completed. There are reports due by the end of the day. Daily activities need to be completed. Robert starts the day by assigning priority to each task.

The presentation is next week and can be completed later. It earns a C. The reports are urgent and need to be completed now. They earn an A. The daily activities need to be completed today, but can be recovered in the morning if they can't get to them. They earn a B. Therefore, throughout the day, Robert completes his reports and most of his daily activities.

He walks away from the day satisfied with his work and knows that tomorrow morning he will complete the daily activities he missed. His day is efficient and productive. No deadlines are missed.

17. 80/20 Rule

The 80/20 rule is used throughout business. It states that 80% of the results come from 20% of the input. It is also known as the **Pareto principle**. The idea is that you can receive the best results if you understand these numbers.   Once you understand the concept, you avoid tasks, ideas, activities, that contribute to the 80% which does not produce the most beneficial effect.

Let's say that you want to increase your sales. The principle states that 80% of your sales originate from 20% of your customers. Therefore, target your attempts towards those accounts included in that 20%. Any advantages, progress, completion, or success will affect 80% of the outcome.
The concept helps you to focus on the tasks that matter the most. It's a way to constantly stay in connection with your goal without losing efficiency and productivity. Once you understand the principle, you can use it to identify your key aspects of any business.

Here's an example of overlooking the 80/20 rule.

Robert has a new sales job. He is looking at all of his customers to assess what strategy he can employ to increase sales in the territory. He has a list that details his customers from greatest sales to smallest. He starts by visiting and assessing the accounts that are closest to him.

The sales of these accounts are small and somewhat insignificant. After visiting a handful of these accounts, he makes the decision to push a certain line heavier than the others. Six months later, his sales are assessed. They have hardly changed at all. Robert is required to look at his accounts and start over.

Here's an example of making the 80/20 rule work.

Robert has a new sales job. He is looking at all of these customers to assess what strategy he can employ to increase sales in the territory. He has a list that details his customers from greatest sales to smallest. He changes his technique by using the 80/20 rule.

The top 20% of his customer list are the ones that become his priority. He visits them all, and through discussion finds what product they are most craving. He pushes that product throughout his accounts visit and is surprised to find that his sales have increased rather quickly and effortlessly.

18. Keep Educated

There are certain careers which mandate continuing education. However, all careers should include continuing education. All industries and businesses change over time. It's true that there are consistent aspects, but it's more important to keep up with the things that adapt and develop. This can be new equipment, new policies, or new regulations. Regardless of the changes, it's important to stay up to date. The job market is terribly competitive. Having the most current knowledge will prove valuable to any prospective employer.

It is also impressive to current employers. The education can make a company more productive. Knowledge of new policies or technology may reduce extra steps that a company may decide to take. It's also possible to prepare for a future position with continuing education. The lack of experience may be overlooked if you present yourself with the knowledge and education credit to back up your skills.

Continuing education can come from many different places. It's possible to go to school. You can join an organization associated with the industry. The organization may provide webinars, publications, or web stories that keep employees up to date. To gain the most from that education, make sure that you practice the skills you learn.

19. Find Motivation

A lack of motivation can cause employees to put forth little effort in their work. They may avoid the workplace, causing unnecessary call offs. Their work may be of lower quality. A business would rather have someone that is productive, creative, and reliable. That type of person requires motivation. Motivation is the thing that makes people enjoy and want to complete tasks. So, what motivates people to be productive? Some people need change to motivate them. Start with a little and the creative juices start flowing.

The beginning of change empowers them to think of all the possibilities. Goals keep a person motivated. It gives them direction and something to look forward to. Accountability keeps people motivated by knowing the consequences of missing their mark. Believe it or not, one of the best sources of motivation is each other. Finding the right leader within an organization to keep people motivated is priceless.

Here are examples of using motivation in an nonfunctional manner.

Robert notices that the reports he is working to complete weekly are redundant. They can be completed more efficiently using their system. He goes to his boss to let him know of his idea. His boss listens to the idea and tells Robert that there is no room for change. He needs to complete the reports as requested if he like his job. This is using accountability for motivation. However, it is also pressing on Robert's motivation, self-esteem, and overall attitude. It will be difficult for Robert to be productive for the remainder of the day.

Here is an example of properly using motivation to increase productivity.

Robert notices that the reports he is working to complete weekly are redundant. They can be completed more efficiently using their system. He goes to his boss to let him know of his idea. His boss listens to the idea and tells Robert that his idea is great.

He asks him to send the details in an email and meet with the IT department to finalize the details. At the end of the day, the boss sends out an email announcing the new method and thanking Robert for his efforts. Robert is now motivated to come forward with new ideas.

He is more motivated to work harder for words of praise from his boss. The documented acknowledgment will serve as a wonderful tool to show future employers of his work ethic.

20. Sleeping Habits

Sleep is needed for the best level of productivity. It's an easy thing to overlook. Getting a good night's rest increases your energy levels for the next day. When a person is tired, it is harder to focus. The work that is produced will most likely be of a lesser quality. It becomes easier to procrastinate when you're tired. When you are exhausted, you will not be productive.

The average person needs 7-9 hours of sleep to be at their top performance. When you plan your time out, it's important to include an adequate amount of sleep also. You will also need to include a small amount of time to get to sleep. Some people need to find a certain way of blowing off steam. It's easy to lie down at night and let your mind run rampant. If you do not account for that time, it cuts into your sleep time. You will end up tired and unproductive.

Here are some ideas for improving your sleep habits. Try using a sleep mask to block out interruptions. Keep light and sound to a minimum. Be consistent about when you go to bed and your bedtime routine. Avoid eating and drinking before your bedtime. Sleep in an area that is comfortable. This means finding the right temperature, the right mattress, and the right pillow.

21. Give a Pat on the Back

It's important to keep people happy. Praise and the recognition of good work can increase productivity. The praise and recognition serves as positive reinforcement. When we reward someone for doing a job well done or completing a task at a higher level, they are more likely to repeat that performance. When we have created the habit of being positive and appreciative, more doors will open.

Receiving praise and compliments also raises a person's self-esteem. When people feel good about themselves, they use that positive energy in the work they do. This is an internal motivational source that can continue to provide performance. Today's life has been plagued with a lack of positive feedback. It's easier to find faults and criticize, instead of providing praise. People are always watching for someone to screw up. We are a society that loves a train-wreck.

Here are some ideas to start giving praise instead of criticism:

A. Understand that criticism is a habit. It may be a habit, but it might be challenging to break.
B. Find appreciation in your own life. The old saying, "Treat others as you would want to be treated" is true. When we criticize others, we may need to understand how hard we are on ourselves.
C. Understand the difference between negative criticism and constructive criticism. In business, constructive criticism is very helpful. You can point out someone's fault or mistakes. However, input or ideas should provide examples of how to move forward. If you are pointing out faults just to inform them, hurt or belittle

them, that would be negative and a waste of time. You lose out on time, productivity, or more.

D. Be natural. You don't want to weird people out. Don't go overboard and start complimenting everyone on every aspect of their life. Give credit where credit is due.

E. Identify when you have negative thoughts or feelings. Take a moment to try and turn your thoughts around. Identify what is good about the situation.

Here's an example of overlooking encouragement and praise.

Robert has been working for a company for several years. He is very good at his job. His boss has come to ask him to complete a special project. The project will require some hours of work at home. Robert works hard and completes the project quickly and with good quality. When he turns the project in, Robert's boss is very dismissive and gives no feedback.

Robert returns to his desk. He starts to think of all the things he missed out on to finish this project. He stayed home during a family gathering because he needed to finish the project. His mind goes from being proud of his results to feeling like a tool that his company used. He vows to no longer accept additional tasks. He will give the most effort within working hours. If he is asked to complete a larger project, he will ask for additional time.

22. The Two Minute Rule

The two-minute rule is a good strategy to use if you want to ward off procrastination. Start by estimating the amount of time it takes to complete a task. If the task takes less than two minutes, get up and do it. There are too many easy items that we avoid for no reason at all. The idea that you get up and move can prove to be motivation to keep going. Remember the old saying, "Items in motion remain in motion. Items at rest tend to remain at rest. The same goes for us. We need something to get us up and moving. When you have a big journey to travel on, start with a small step. In the end, a big journey is nothing more than a lot of small steps...

Since the small items are typically what we blow off, completing them will free our to-do list for more deserving items. If someone follows this rule, they will be less tempted to fall into a lazy category or continue to procrastinate. Plus it's easy to spare two minutes.

Here is an example of properly using the two minute rule.

Robert arrives to work. He sits down and starts to write down all the tasks he needs to complete. He adds them to his already existing list. When he adds things in, he applies the two-minute rules and notices that there are some tasks he can complete without adding them onto his list.

Once his list is finished, he has already completed several tasks without thinking about it. This helps to make his list more manageable. It also helps to gain momentum with his work. He already has the flow of completing tasks going.

23. Multi-tasking – Big No, No...

Multi-tasking used to be the hidden treasure of abilities. Studies have revealed the truth about multi-tasking. We can now categorize it as a bad habit that we want to avoid. The art of multi-tasking has been proven to be less productive. This is because the brain does not switch between tasks effectively and we are much more likely to make mistakes when multi-tasking.

In today's world, we are always trying to multitask. The biggest offenders are usually smart phone users. It has become impossible to disconnect from the millions of distractions out in the world. We read our emails while having lunch with a long lost friend. We are texting people while we are driving our kids to school. We answer phone calls while standing at a cash register.

We can eliminate multi-tasking. But you need to start by prioritizing. Make sure you can recognize that distractions are just that...distractions. When a block of time is assigned to a task, make sure that the block of time is void of all intruders. Do not answer phone calls, emails, or start to surf the internet, unless those are the tasks you are planning to achieve.

24. Consider Going Digital

Technology has developed numerous ways of improving business productivity. There are programs that keep track of inventory, sales, receipts, or templates. Businesses have come to accept technology as an imperative part of the needed tools. However, in startup businesses or older family businesses, it may be harder to implement the new tools.

Paper records can increase mistakes. They can get lost or damaged easily. They make transactions quicker and more accurate.

Here are some examples of improving productivity through technology. When companies are spread out throughout other areas, technology can allow meetings over teleconferences. It makes it easier to talk to those off the grounds. There are programs that can create and track to-do lists. Some of these programs will allow sharing of task lists. A company will need less space to keep their records. Paper trails require storage, which can be unproductive. Technology allows the team to collaborate even when they are apart.

25. Take Breaks

Studies show regular breaks improve your productivity and creativity. If you skip breaks, you can get more stressed out and exhausted. The brain is like any other muscle. If you try and use it for a prolonged amount of time, it can become fatigued and give a poor performance. However, if you give it a chance to rest, you are more likely to have better results. Taking a break is a way of recharging your brain.

People usually skip breaks because of guilt. There are times when a break can be counterproductive. Do not take a break if you have momentum going. It is estimated that only 1 in 3 people actually take their breaks and it's becoming more and more common to eat lunch at your desk.

It's only necessary for micro breaks every 15 minutes or so. These micro breaks do not require you to leave your workplace. They are 30 seconds long. These breaks reduce fatigue by 50%. It has been documented that breaks increase productivity by 6.45%.

After a sensible break, you will be more productive. You'll return to your work more creative and open-minded. Decisions will be easier and less stressful. You should find a comfortable place to take longer breaks that allows you to escape from the noises and the sounds of your work.

26. Find Love and Fun in Your Work

The fact is that if we are having fun we are happy. Conducting work in an environment where we are happy helps to improve our self-talk. It helps to motivate us to do a good job. Employees that are happy are less likely to call off sick. Working in a fun environment actually produces less complaints and can encourage a more creative mindset. It can also help to retain employees.

It is important to keep a good balance of fun. Too much fun can be counterproductive. The fun should be work related and it needs to be done in a way that doesn't cause distraction to other workers. In addition to being more productive and creative, fun can be used as a reward for a job well done.

Finding a job in things that you love will help to hold you accountable for your tasks. If you are personally invested in your work, you are more likely to meet deadlines. You are more likely to put effort and detail in the outcome. Another term for the love of the job is passion. With passion, comes a greater performance. Passionate people are more engaged. Someone who is passionate about their work is always looking for a challenge.

Here are some examples for making work fun. One way to involve people and make things more fun is to encourage the employees to share their ideas. It helps to become personally invested in the job. Being dependent increases self-esteem and makes people happy, so try creating a fun team. They are responsible for hosting fun events to bring together everyone.

They don't have to take up too much time or money either. One of the events could be a cubicle decorating contest for the holidays. The winner is then awarded with a gift card or something like that. By letting customers know how much fun it is to work at your organization, this can also help with boosting your business's reputation.

27. Keep Momentum

Momentum is important for a person's willpower and productivity. There is a negative and a positive momentum. Negative momentum is harmful to productivity. Positive momentum is incredible for productivity. Negative momentum happens when someone starts out with doing nothing.

There are moments when sitting on the couch for prolonged amounts of time make it harder and harder to get up and go somewhere. The longer you sit, the harder it gets to make that first step to being productive. Cut out the negative momentum. Start by looking at the few past hours. Assess what you have accomplished. Take yourself back to the present moment and push to move forward. Do not beat yourself up for time that cannot be returned.

Positive momentum has to start with a push. You need to make that first step and get moving. Once you make that first move, it becomes easier to build more momentum. Along the way, reward yourself. Try and make the positive momentum a habit. Be consistent with that habit. Pat yourself on the back for getting up and pushing forward. Take breaks along the way, but be careful not to fall back into that negative momentum.

Here's an example of negative momentum causing a problem with productivity.

Robert has worked for the past few hours. It is lunchtime and the team has organized a potluck. Robert goes to the cafeteria. He starts talking with other employees. After 15 minutes, he grabs his food and sits down. After eating and conversing, another 30 minutes has passed.

He looks at the clock and knows that he should return to his desk but he doesn't want to leave the situation. After 15 more minutes, he gets up and returns to his desk. He looks over the work that remains and determines that he doesn't have enough time left to finish today anyways.

He spends some time surfing the internet and answering a few emails. Finally the day ends and Robert has accomplished half the work he normally does.

28. Exercise

Exercise boosts your productivity. It is known that regular exercise makes people happy, healthy, and energetic. Exercise is known to sharpen a person's mind. A regular exercise routine will allow you more energy throughout the day. It doesn't happen instantaneously. It will take a few weeks before a person starts to feel the benefits of exercising regularly. Regular exercise has been known to allow people to be more tolerant of themselves and each other.

Studies have been conducted that show that finding an exercise program midday provides the best results in productivity. There are a few different options that companies can do. Some offices have a gym in them. It's also becoming increasingly common for employees to take a walk during their lunch.

Exercise allows alertness. The blood flow to the brain is increased. The energy you gain helps to assure that you performing at your best. You will be less likely to make mistakes. You will have the energy to put full potential into your work. You should aim for 30 minutes of exercise at least 5 days a week.

Exercising regularly helps you maintain your energy. It keeps you alert. By being fit and healthy you are also less likely to get sick, which decreases the amount of sick days you take in general.

29. Avoid Distractions

To keep distractions out of your work, you should focus on yourself. Keep away from multi-tasking. It's just working on several distractions at one time. Instead focus on one item. Be careful about getting addicted to emails.

Schedule times for checking your email. Let's face it. Incoming emails occur all day long. If you answer every one at the time it arrives, you will never have time for completing tasks. Turn away from social media. Sometimes the fastest way to get an answer is to pick up the phone and ask. Sending an email or text can waste time and effort.

Distractions can be external or internal. It is up to you to find a way to stay focused on the task you are completing. Stressful situations may be playing in your head. You may have brought home to work with you. There may be some curiosity that is pulling you away from your task. No matter what it is, recognize it for the real thing it is; a distraction.

Here are examples of office distractions:

    A. Loud appliances
    B. Inadequate temperatures
    C. The internet
    D. Social coworkers
    E. Uncomfortable chairs and desks

30. Learn Keyboard Shortcuts

The computer is a tool that is present in almost every business in the 21st Century. There are so many levels of expertise out there, that the use of pen and paper has almost been made redundant. In businesses, we usually use the same functions every day.

Each time we set up in front of it, we are geared to use a function that we may have used a million times before. Is there anyway to be more efficient about that? Of course there is. The wonderful software makers have created shortcuts in many programs. The shortcuts are meant to save time and make regular functions easier. However, we don't always use the shortcuts that are available to us.

Here are some examples of common program shortcuts:

A. Windows
- a. F1 – Help
- b. CTRL + Esc – Opens the Start Menu
- c. Alt + Tab – Flip between open programs
- d. Shift + Delete – Delete an item

B. Web browsers
- a. Ctrl + N – Opens a new window
- b. Ctrl + T – Opens a new tab
- c. Ctrl + R – Refreshes the window
- d. Esc – Stops
- e. Alt + Home PG – Goes to the homepage

C. The Clipboard
- a. Ctrl +C – Copy selection

b. Ctrl + O – Open an existing document
c. Ctrl + W – Closes the existing document
d. Ctrl + S – Saves the current documents
e. Ctrl + P – Prints the current document

31. Establish Rewards

Rewards are a valuable tool for increasing productivity. It requires a reward that is satisfying to the employees. If there is a reward which has little meaning, it can actually hurt productivity. It not only hurts productivity, it also wastes time and money. When finding the appropriate reward, it's important to make sure that the reward is measurable.

There are different types of rewards. The most obvious is money. Money is a very motivating tool for people. Connect the reward with a specific accomplishment. Praise is a great reward. It costs nothing and gains a lot. It has to be tied to the performance. Therefore, make sure that recognition is private and public.

Rewards can also be given for team performance. A reward system may create a cohesive unity among the workplace. When people are functioning as a team, it is proven to be productive. A business will also want to make sure that the reward is targeted at long-term results. This will insure that you get the best results out of your reward system. Employees or you will push for the long-term each and every day.

Do not just consider the employer rewarding the employee. Remember that as an employee, you may need to reward yourself sometimes. This improves your own productivity. Consider buying yourself something. It's a way to have a souvenir of your accomplishment. Another reward is to pamper you.

That can be in the form of a massage, new hairdo, or more. Some will choose to take some time off. If you had some extra hours completing a task and your mind has been focused on nothing but your work, you deserve a break. Therefore you might want to consider planning a vacation.

32. Use Automation

Automation is a great way to increase productivity. Automation increases speed, accuracy, and the ability to share information. If something is automated, it is usually more consistent. This will help employees to inspect the information or process involved in the task. It takes the originality out of the product.

The use of automation will cut down a to-do list. There will no longer need to be reminders or managing mistakes. It frees up time for higher priority items that call for more micromanaging.

Here are examples of when to automate:

   A. If it's possible to automate, do it.
   B. If the task is simple and redundant

33. Travel Efficiently

Traveling has become a part of many businesses. It's very easy to lose momentum and productivity while traveling. There are challenges that are specific to being away from the business that hurt productivity. Traveling is not an opportunity to relax and take a break. Sometimes we think of it as a vacation because there is a change of scenery.

Travel needs to be well planned. Business travel is not the time to make spur of the moment decisions. Poor planning can cost the business money and efficiency. Since you are away from your usual place of business, it's important to plan to have access to the tools you need while you travel. Find a way to stay connected to those still at work. There are many different ways, such as email, texts, or phone calls.

Here are examples of how traveling can harm productivity:

A. Taking care of you may become more difficult. It's easier to eat food that tastes good but is not healthy when on the road. It can also cause a disturbance to your usual exercise routine.
B. You may miss out on regular schedule activities because of your absence. For example, perhaps there is an email that you routinely send out on the day that you travel.
C. There is a possibility that you may not have an internet connection while you travel. It can be difficult finding a good Wi-Fi or hot spot connection.
D. The additional noise and bustle from a new environment may be very distracting to your focus while traveling.

E. You may be used to using your tools that are on hand at work. During travel, these tools may not be accessible, which causes tasks to take longer.

Here are examples of making sure you are productive while traveling:

A. Planning ahead will make use of every second of your day.
B. Delegating tasks that you will be unavailable to complete will keep the business productive and keep tasks from building up upon your return.
C. Find the right electronic device that can access the information you need for your travel.
D. Find ways to move through airports quickly. This may mean you have to pack light and avoid checking your luggage. It may be more productive to catch a cab rather than wait for a ride.
E. Stocking your devices with information that can be accessible without an internet connection allows you to use your time to review or work on tasks during moments without the internet.

34. Stay Up to Date

Staying up to date in the business world can be quite cumbersome. It's important to stay up to date on new regulations. It's important to stay up to date on technology. It's also important to stay up to date on business changes.

There are many different things that can help keep a person or group up to date. A person should receive updates from their employer, but they should also hold themselves accountable for keeping themselves up to date.
Staying up to date increases productivity. Imagine the time and effort wasted on data or projects that are outdated.

Keeping up to date can save time, money, and effort. There are publications available for many business fields. There are news articles that provide information on certain topics. Businesses should be conducting meetings that are productive and information should be shared in a reliable and consistent manner with others.

Here is an example of how not staying up to date can hurt a company's productivity.

Robert is visited by an employee for corporate. They are conducting an inspection regarding a specific committee that Robert is responsible for. The employee asks for the meeting minutes. The minutes are in a binder. They are organized and detailed. The employee looks them over and shakes his head. The meeting minutes need to be redone, all of them.

The format that Robert has been using is outdated. Over a year ago, the company switched to a new format which includes new information required by certain accreditations. The lack of informed keeping caused Robert additional work. He now has to redo all of his work. In addition to that, he may be missing information that should be within the notes.

Here is an example of staying up to date and how it can increase productivity. Robert is visited by an employee for corporate business. They are conducting an inspection regarding a specific committee that Robert is responsible for.

The employee asks for the meeting minutes. The minutes are in a binder. They are organized and detailed. The format matches the update that was sent to Robert a year ago. In addition, Robert has checked accreditation details throughout the year and added information that needed to be added.

35. Training

Training has a direct correlation between productivity and employee retention. It is easy to cut training when budgets need to be tightened. The companies that are productive and successful see the value in training their employees. Training should be considered to be a benefit to employees. It is not a requirement. The time and money invested in training is expected to pay off in productivity and efficiency.

Training helps individuals meet their personal goals and organizations meet their goals as well. Proper training frees management from having to troubleshoot and micromanage employee tasks. It makes it easier for employees to handle questions and request on the spot, instead of passing the issue on to another person. That improves customer satisfaction. The increase in independence also helps to build the management-employee relationships.

Here's an example of a lack of training hurting productivity:

Robert is asked to sit at the front desk. It is not his common position, but the person who normally covers the position is out sick. His manager says that it is easy enough. All he needs to do is sit and answer any questions from customers that come in.

The first customer comes in and approaches the desk. The customer would like to see a specific employee. Robert picks up the phone and calls the employee. The employee says that she will be right there.

On the way to see the customer, the employee stops at the manager's office and complains that you interrupted her work for a customer without an appointment. The employee continues to the front desk and meets with the customer.

After several minutes, the manager calls and states that there should be no customers meeting with employees without appointments. Momentum was lost from the employee and the manager. The customer was left waiting for a longer amount of time because of the employee approaching the manager. All of the loss in productivity could have been avoided by training.

Here's an example of training improving productivity:
Robert has spent the last week in training seminars for a new service that starts today. He arrives at his desk and takes his first call.

He is prepared for the customers' questions and has prepared materials to answer any questions or concerns. His manager is not involved in any interactions. The customers are answered without any delay and Robert is confident in answering all requests.

36. Change

Our goal is to be productive and efficient. If we are looking to change the outcome of our work style or business practice, we also have to change the way we do the things that produce that outcome. Change does not have to be earth shattering, some of the smallest changes can make the biggest difference.

When we look to change things, we have to look from small too big. Start with changing your own work habits or space. Let the target get a little bigger. Focus on the team that you work with. Introduce the reasons why change is needed. Show that there is a benefit to implementing the change. Look at your department or area of expertise. Consider the changes and propose them to the ones that need to hear about it. Look at the organization as a whole.

Make sure that every change you make has a way of monitoring the effects. Be prepared to acknowledge whether it is a positive or negative effect on productivity. People are not always open to change. It does not come natural because we are creatures of habit. We like the way that we have always done things. It comes easy and feels right. We have to make sure that people, or ourselves, are motivated to follow through on the needed changes.

Here are some examples of why we resist change:

A. Fear
B. Lack of knowledge
C. The wrong information
D. Our past
E. Threat to our status
F. We do not have the sight of the benefit
G. Lack of trust

H. Afraid of looking bad
I.   Unwillingness to risk things
J. A difficulty to abandon old habits

Increasing productivity during periods of resistance requires understanding why the resistance is there in the first place. Once you identify the reason, it will be easier to overcome and move forward with the change. The best way to implement change is to provide as much information as possible while highlighting the benefits.

37. Avoid Paper Clutter

It's funny how much paper clutter we still collect, especially since we are such a technology driven world. Paper clutter comes from mail, work, publications, catalogues, receipts, or newspapers.

When you find yourself surrounded by paper clutter, start with evaluating where it is coming from. Find out why you don't have a place for it. Maybe you need more drawers or files to keep that stuff in. See if they are things that you need. Maybe there is a publication subscription that could be canceled because it isn't being used.

Try looking to see if catalogues are available online. If they are, cut down on the paper and try to use the online store. For the types of paper you want to keep, find a place to store them. Sort through everything and determine if you want to keep it, recycle it, or throw it away. The things you keep should be labeled. Place post it notes as to what you would like to read or to mark pages that are important.

Having paper clutter creates a black hole for things to hide in. This may make it hard to find work when you need it. Paper clutter can build up to hazardous levels. If you have ever entered an office with stacks of paper laying everywhere, you know what I mean. Getting rid of the clutter will allow you to find things easier. You will be able to keep track of things better. You may remember where something is now, but can anyone find it in you absence?

Here's an example of paper clutter causing unproductive results.

Robert arrives at work to find the piles of paper he left behind the day before. He starts the day with a sense of stress and panic. When his computer starts, he reads an email about a presentation that is needed for a customer proposal. He knows that he has it. It's somewhere in the pile. He has to spend one hour of his day shuffling through papers to find the presentation. He has wasted time and effort because of his paper clutter.

Here's an example of managing paper clutter to have a productive situation.

Robert arrives at work to find his clear desk from the previous day. He starts his computer and finds an email regarding a presentation that is needed for a customer presentation. The presentation is sitting in the appropriate file and Robert takes his copy to his boss. The whole task is completed in 5 minutes. No time or effort was wasted.

38. Use Templates

There are many common programs that businesses use to put together forms. Items, like faxes, letters, letterheads and more, are used on a daily basis. It can be time consuming to constantly add in the same information every time. It wastes time and effort to not utilize some type of templates.

The use of templates will eliminate mistakes. It will save time. It will make productivity better. It will be more efficient for workers. It will also make certain tasks less intimidating to employees to complete.

Here are some ideas of when to use templates:

    A. Job descriptions
    B. Letters to customers
    C. Fax Cover Sheets
    D. Profit and Loss Reports
    E. Standard Agreements
    F. Employee Reviews
    G. Incident Reports
    H. Any Type of Document that is used regularly

39. Create Deadlines

Deadlines are a person's way of establishing accountability for our work. It helps to divert our bad habit of procrastinating. Deadlines need to be realistic to be productive. Creating a deadline is a way of budgeting your time. It gives us incentive to complete tasks on time.

When a person efficiently uses deadlines they are more productive. They have a better work ethic. They are continuously moving toward their goals. Achieving your work before your deadline gives a sense of satisfaction. Deadlines also help to keep a person's schedule from getting too tight.

When you create your deadline, set aside blocks of time. Make sure that you include a small cushion of time for any surprises or delays. Once you reach your deadline and have completed your task, find a way to celebrate. It doesn't have to be a big celebration.You can choose something small, like acknowledging with a smile is big enough.

Here's an example of using a timeline to work productively:

Robert is leading an organizational meeting. At the end of the meeting, he is announcing all the things that need to be accomplished before the next one. He has delegated each one.

After assigning each task, he labels each one with a deadline. There is some information regarding quarterly data. That will be due by the next quarter. There is information about the past sales. That will be due in 3 weeks.

This gives an additional week, before the next meeting, to analyze the data. At the next meeting, everything is prepared without any stressful procrastination. Each person takes care of their assigned task and turns the information in to Robert.

40. Keep the Right Tools

Obviously, it is very difficult, if not impossible, to complete a task without the proper tools. It is up to a company to provide those tools. However, an employee should request items if they need them. It's just as important to have the right quality of tools. For example, you will need a computer program to download certain information. There are several programs available. Only one provides the reports that include all the data you need. It wouldn't be very productive to utilize any other program.

Time is a tool that people don't often consider. When a task is given, you need to have the right amount of time to complete it. To be productive, a person should know all the tools that will be needed for a task before starting.

They should check to make sure they have access to those tools. If there is anything that is missing, that person should communicate the need to the appropriate person and gather a time when it will become available.

Finally, it's important to take care of those tools and keep them clean and in working order for your own productivity and so that others may utilize the same tools.

41. WADE Formula

The Wade Formula is a method for utilizing good time management. Wade is an acronym that stands for:

A. Write it down.
B. Add things up.
C. Decide to delete, delegate, delay, or diminish any tasks.
D. Execute.

Write down everything that comes to mind. Get all your tasks out of your head. Consider how much time everything will take to complete. Make your decisions as to what you can complete and what you need to complete later. Finally, get to work. Go through your list and get it done.

Here's an example of using the Wade Formula productively.

Robert sits down at his desk for a new day. He has a lot to accomplish in a little bit of time. Over the next week, there is a meeting that he needs to coordinate. There is an agenda to create and manage.

He has to send out invites to the meeting as soon as possible. He has daily items that need completed. He starts to feel overwhelmed. He takes a deep breath and starts writing. He writes everything that needs to be accomplished. He then jots down roughly how much time each item takes. The list still seems too massive for him.

He looks over the list and sees what items can be delegated. There are several items that his partner can complete. There are a few tasks that can be accomplished after the hustle has died down.

Finally, he has a list that he can work with. Robert starts working down the list to accomplish his tasks. By the end of the day, he has completed everything and is in a good state of mind to start fresh the next day.

1. Cross train
2. Be Realistic
3. De-clutter
4. Avoid Over Promising

42. Using a Smartphone

The smartphone has earned a reputation as being very harmful to productivity. However, it has tools that are valuable. There are apps aimed at improving productivity. The smartphone can also give you access to information while you are away. You can get more done quicker. You can keep calendar, to-do lists, and contacts in a central location that are easier to access. Smartphones also allow you to answer emails while away.

When you return to your workplace, you will have less to answer for. Any pressing issues can be answered immediately instead of making the customer or team member wait.

Smartphones also allow people to have mini breaks. Taking the mini breaks help to increase focus. Increased focus amounts to increased productivity.

Here are some common apps designed to increase productivity:

    A. Doodle
    B. Workflowy
    C. GarminFit
    D. Zite
    E. Dropbox
    F. Due
    G. HootSuite

43. Attitude

It is commonly said that your attitude determines the amount of productivity you produce. If you want to get things done, find that good attitude. Make sure that a negative situation does not distract you from the remainder of your tasks and work. It is easy to let drama or negativity drag us down. It stifles our momentum and pushes away from completion.

Not only do YOU need to keep a positive attitude, but you will want to surround yourself with others that have the same.

If you need to change your attitude, start by identifying the reason you have the bad attitude. Find a way o change that situation. Focus on pointing out the positive in any situation. Surround yourself with people that are inspiring.

Here are some examples of how a positive attitude increases productivity.

    A. Keeping a positive attitude makes you more approachable. People are more willing to help.
    B. Complaining is a complete waste of time. Plan ahead and eliminate time wasting by keeping a positive attitude.
    C. A positive attitude is energy building. The increase in energy will increase your productivity.
    D. Your attitude will control your self-talk, which can help build confidence when you need it.
    E. Having a good attitude can make a bad situation less troublesome. Approaching a problem with a bad attitude usually builds negativity.

44. Keep Meetings Productive

Meetings have the possibility of being very productive or an incredible waste of time. There are many ways to keep a meeting productive. Make sure that you have valid points to talk about. Conclude each meeting with action points that need to be completed.

A creative option is to make meetings standing only. Keep everyone from sitting. This helps to keep everyone more focused. If there is a spur of the moment meeting, it should be specific. The topic should take no more than 10 minutes. Start a meeting by explaining the purpose of the gathering.

Meetings have the potential to be very damaging to productivity. Meetings are distractions to completing tasks. If a meeting runs too long you lose the focus of those attending. Inviting people that do not have any relationship with the topic decreases productivity. Decisions can be made without the people that need to sign off on the action. This accomplishes nothing.

Here are steps to hosting a productive meeting:

A. Make sure that you know everyone that is attending and that they are relevant to the content.
B. Do a lot of listening and less speaking. This will allow people to feel free to give their opinions.
C. Keep the meeting on time. Start it at the right moment and finish at the specified time.
D. Keep notes or have someone keep detailed notes about the meeting.
E. Keep things interesting and positive.

45. Build Morale

Morale is an important part of productivity. If the employees of a workplace are enthusiastic and happy, they are more willing to work as a team. They feel a need to accomplish more. The relationships between workers will become more positive. A place with a higher morale tends to have more respectful employees. It is also known that places with higher morale have a higher rate of retaining their employees.

If a company or employer takes the time to build morale, employees will be more loyal and productive for the company. Morale can be ruined very easy. There are certain people that thrive in destroying morale. It can suffer from rumors, drama, scandals, and complainers. As an individual, we can decide to strive for building good morale by avoiding these things.

Here are some ways to boost morale:

A. Celebrate the holidays and large events together. Make sure that no one is excluded.
B. Develop a reward program for those being productive.
C. Keep the environment clean, comfortable, and pleasant to look at.
D. Smile. They are said to be contagious.
E. Trust in people and make sure that you someone they can trust.
F. Show that you are having fun.

Conclusion

Productivity is very important to every employee and employer. It means that you giving the most output with the least amount of waste. To be productive, you have to recognize what is not productive. You need to find the areas that need to be changed.

Changes can be hard to enforce. Personal change can be met with hesitation and fear. Throughout this book, you have been faced with 45 different ways to boost productivity. You do not need to change everything all at once. Start with a few items and see how they work. Every situation is unique and may require unique strategies.

Increasing productivity is not the job of one person. Any organization should be working together to increase productivity. If each person is doing their share of the work, collectively there is no chance of failure.

Consider the way you spend your time, money, and resources while doing your work. Find out where improvement can be made and do it. Take the steps to becoming a better person, employee, or employer using these strategies – and watch as your business success continues to grow.

www.ingramcontent.com/pod-product-compliance
Lightning Source LLC
Chambersburg PA
CBHW071620170526
45166CB00003B/1122